New Hampshire

Unforgettable Vintage Images of the Granite State

Note from the Publisher

Royalties from the sale of this book will be paid into a fund for historic preservation to be administered by Arcadia Publishing. We envisage that proceeds from the fund will go toward supporting local history projects in the community. For further details, please contact us at Arcadia's Midwest office.

NEW HAMPSHIRE

Unforgettable Vintage Images of the Granite State

ARCADIA

First published 2000.

Published by:
Tempus Publishing, Inc.
3047 N. Lincoln Ave., Suite 410
Chicago, IL 60657

Typesetting and orginination by Tempus Publishing, Inc.
Printed and bound in Great Britain.

Library of Congress Number: 00-105698
ISBN 0-7385-0754-7

For all general information contact Arcadia Publishing at:
Telephone 843-853-2070
Fax 843-853-0044
E-Mail sales@arcadiapublishing.com

For customer service and orders:
Toll-Free 1-888-313-2665

Visit us on the internet at http://www.arcadiapublishing.com

CONTENTS

ACKNOWLEDGMENTS

Arcadia would like the thank the following authors for their contributions:

E. John B. Allen — *New England Skiing*

James Dolph — *Around Portsmouth in the Victorian Era*

Ronan Donohoe — *Around Portsmouth in the Victorian Era*

David Emerson — *The Conways*
White Mountain Hotels, Inns, and Taverns

Farmington Historical Society — *Farmington*

Bruce D. Heald, Ph. D. — *Railways and Waterways Through the White Mountains*
The Boats and Ports of Lake Winnepesaukee
The Lakes Region of New Hampshire Volume 1
The Lakes Region of New Hampshire Volume ll

Mabel Hidden — *The Lower Mount Washington Valley*

Thom Hindle — *Dover*

Thomas A. House — *Durham: A Century of Photographs*

Warren D. Huse — *Lakeport*
Laconia

Richard N. Johnson — *Around Jackson*

Helen LaFave — *Stratham*

Arthur F. March Jr. — *Littleton*

Renney E. Morneau — *Berlin*

William E. Ross — *Durham: A Century of Photographs*

Alan F. Rumrill — *Keene*
J.A. French's Cheshire County

Robert B. Stephenson — *The Towns of the Monadnock Region*

William H. Teschek — *Hampton and Hampton Beach*

Jean Ulitz — *The Lower Mount Washington Valley*

William M. Varrell — *Rye and Rye Beach*

Arcadia would like the thank the following historical societies for their contributions

Albany Historical Society
Alton Historical Society
Androscoggin Valley Hospital
Appalachian Mountain Club
Bear Island Conservation Association
Belmont Historical Society
Berlin and Coos County Historical Society
Berlin Fire Department
Berlin Police Department
Berlin Public Library
Boston Public Library
Centre Harbor Historical Society
Conway Historical Society
Conway Public Library
Cook Memorial Library
Dartmouth Outing Club
Dover Heritage Group
Dover Public Library
Dublin Historical Society
Durham Historic Association Museum
Earle Wells Collection
Fitzwilliam Historical Society
Geneva Point Center
Gorham Historical Society
Hancock Historical Society
Historic Harrisville, Inc.
Historical Society of Cheshire County
Holy Trinity School
Jaffrey Center Village Improvement Society
Laconia Historical Society
Laconia Museum Society, Inc.
Laconia Public Library
Lake Winnipesaukee Historical Society
Lakes Region Association
Lane Memorial Library
Littleton Area Historical Society

Littleton Historic Museum
Marlborough Historical Society
Meredith Historical Society
Mount Washington Observatory, Inc.
Moutonboro Historical Society
New England Ski Museum in Franconia
NH Antique & Classic Boat Museum
NH Dpt. of Environmental Services
NH Fish & Game Department
NH Highway Department
NH Historical Society
NH Planning & Development Commission
New Ipswich Historical Society
Ossippee Historical Society
Portsmouth Anthenaeum
Portsmouth Herald
Portsmouth Historical Society
Rindge Historical Society
Society for the Protection of New Hampshire
South Baptist Church of Laconia
Sterling & Francine Clark Art Institute
Stratham Historical Society
Tamworth Historical Society
Trustees and Librarians of Goodwin Library
Tuck Museum
Tuftonboro Historical Society
Union Hall Association
United Baptist Church of Lakeport
White Mountain National Forest
Winnipesaukee Flagship Corporation
Wolfeboro Historical Society
Woodman Institute

INTRODUCTION

Nature's first green is gold,
Her hardest hue to hold.
Her early leaf's a flower;
But only so an hour.
Then leaf subsides to leaf.
So Eden sank to grief,
So dawn goes down to day.
Nothing gold can stay.

- "Nothing Gold Can Stay," Robert Frost

Every land has a poet, and every poet a land. Boston has Poe, Chicago has Sandburg, New York has Hughes, but never have a poet and a land been such a perfect match as New Hampshire and Robert Frost. Frost knew that America is not in the courtrooms of Boston, the commercialism of New York City, nor is America in the bricks of Independence Hall or the grassy field of Gettysberg; America is in the water of Lake Winnipesaukee, in the peaks and valleys of the White Mountains, and in the shores of the New Hampshire coast. Maybe Robert Frost was right when he wrote that "nothing gold can stay," but as long as the sun rises and falls, a New Hampshire sunset is just about as close to gold as one can get.

The romanticism of the Granite State has been forever intertwined in the reality of politics. Every four years, the country's attention turns to the New Hampshire primary: the first, and arguably, the most important primary during the presidential election year. More so than a predeterminer for the upcoming election, the primary reminds Americans that democracy is in the hands of the people. New Hampshire was the first state to declare its independence from England as well as the first state to require its constitution to refer to its citizens for approval. For a state whose motto is "Live Free or Die," New Hampshirites truly understand the freedom that so many sons and daughters gave their lives for over the violent two hundred years of American history.

Of the eight books in the "Best of" series, the "Best of New Hampshire" holds, more than any other, a special place in the heart of Arcadia. While Arcadia celebrates the publication of its 1,000th book, the 999 books which followed *Dover, New Hampshire* would never have been produced had that first *Images of America* book found an audience. Seven years and two more offices later, Dover and New Hampshire are still considered Arcadia's home. The passion, generosity, and just plain love of their state from historical societies and the authors have not only inspired Arcadia to grow, it has left an ever-lasting impression on all those who work for and have worked for Arcadia. There's no one else we would rather celebrate our 1,000th book than with the great state of New Hampshire.

Mike Spiegel
Editor, Arcadia Publishing

One
FACES AND PLACES

Joseph Barnard and a fine Jersey bull in front of the Captain Hoitt's farm. This had been the site of the town poor farm on Heights Road near Elton Avenue. The bull has brass knobs on the horns, a decoration as well as a safety feature to keep the bull from charging and possibly hurting a person. (Stratham Historical Society.)

Paul Gowen Chase and his mother, Bertha Gowen Chase. Mother and son are feeding the piglets at the Chase Farm on Bunker Hill Avenue in Stratham, *c.* 1912. (Helen Chase.)

Automobile Club, *c.* 1912. This group of New Hampshire motorists, touring the White Mountains in identical automobiles, posed before the Kearsarge House, North Conway.

Astronomers predicted that the best spot to view the 1932 eclipse was in the Conway-Fryeburg area. Preparations were made for a huge throng of eclipse viewers. Restaurants hired extra workers and a viewing ground was set up behind the high school. The throngs appeared as predicted with no reports of panic or pandemonium.

An early view of the north side of Central Street taken from in front of the Steamboat Hotel in Farmington.

Back when fur coats were a popular item of apparel, the trapping and hunting of animals such as these foxes shot by Charles Wyatt (on right) and friend provided a seasonal means of income.

Albert D. Littlehale (right) and extension agent T.R. Arkell examine a sheep, 1910. In later years, it was not uncommon for Littlehale to herd his flock down Main Street Durham.

Oren V. "Dad" Henderson with his chickens in Durham, *c.* 1925.

A wedding party at Red Tower, June 1901. This image shows the wedding of Edith Angela Congreve (Hamilton Smith's stepdaughter) to Shirley Onderdonk of New York. Mrs. Onderdonk later gave $16,000 toward the construction of Smith Hall, as a memorial to her mother. (Durham Historic Association.)

Mrs. Alice Jennings Congreve Smith, with her granddaughter Alice at Red Tower, *c.* 1905. (Durham Historic Association.)

Professor Frederick W. Taylor and the "Tom Thumb" carriage, early 1920s. This English-made carriage was given to Mr. and Mrs. Tom Thumb, the famous circus couple, by Queen Victoria. It came to the University of New Hampshire as a memorial to Maxwell Smalley of Walpole, New Hampshire. Taylor later gave it to the Henry Ford Museum in Dearborn, Michigan.

The faculty of the University of New Hampshire in Dover in 1899. From left to right are: (seated) Fred W. Morse, professor of organic chemistry; Charles H. Waterhouse, instructor in dairying; Herbert H. Lamson, associate professor of botany; Charles H. Pettee, dean and professor of mathematics and civil engineering; President of the College Charles Sumner Murkland, professor of English language and literature; Clarence M. Weed, professor of zoology and entomology; Frank W. Rane, professor of horticulture; and Clarence W. Scott, professor of history and political economy; (standing) Frederic S. Johnston, assistant professor of agriculture; Irving A. Colby, instructor in wood work; Arthur F. Nesbit, associate professor of physics and electrical engineering; Charles W. Burkett, professor of agriculture; Charles L. Parsons, professor of general and analytical chemistry; Joseph H. Hawes, associate professor of drawing; Richard Whoriskey Jr., assistant professor of modern languages; and Edward E. Russell, engineer and curator of buildings.

Laurence V. Jensen, the first "Mayor of Durham," 1926. In 1926, the Blue Key, a senior honorary society, sponsored the first "mayoralty" campaign. Jensen's platform promoted individual liberty and was against allowing female matrons in male dormitories.

An early 1900s photograph of the Ladies' Bicycle Club, at the porte cochere of the Laconia passenger station.

A shiny Henderson motorcycle with sidecar and two passengers on Mechanic Street in Keene. Irving L. Kibbee opened his motorcycle and bicycle repair shop in 1915. His son "Red" Kibbee attained considerable local fame as a baseball player.

Santa Claus and his reindeer pose on Mechanic Street before making an appearance at a community Christmas tree observance around 1920. John Chapman dressed as Santa and settled into the converted sidecar of this "Majestic" motorcycle before taking to the snowy streets.

Pictured is the summit of Mt. Agassiz, (alt. 2,369 feet). This mountain, formerly known as Peaked Hill, affords a fine view over the White and Green Mountains. The present name of the mountain was given in honor of Professor Louis Agassiz, whose research of the glacial remains in this vicinity has proven to be of great value.

District Ranger Truman E. Hale (back row, left) and his crew of Boy Scouts improve the Valley Way Trail over the Presidential Range in 1931.

Campers along the Peabody River, Dolly Copp Campground, 1930s.

Adam Drake's coach at Foss' boarding house. The coach, said to have been brown with yellow trim, is about to set off on the morning mail run to Portsmouth. Many of those on the coach are members of the extended Richardson family from Wakefield, Massachusetts.

To quote a local Victorian reporter, "The Bible says that all men are created equal, but when dressed in bathing suits they sure don't look it."

An 1880s camp at Rye, possibly at Rand's Grove off Cable Road.

Gypsies at the Farragut Hotel. The Farragut gypsies, who made and sold sweetgrass baskets and other souvenirs, were a fixture at Rye Beach for many years. They were always remembered as a highly-regarded part of the community.

The U.S. Ski Team, 1955. From left to right are Red McGuire, Dick Binette, Scotty Scott, and Alfredo Mendoza.

Our Boys Drum Corps parade, around the turn of the century, on an unpaved Gold Street, with the railroad track and trestle in the background. Lakeport had a long history of musical organizations, of which Rublee's Band was pre-eminent for several decades.

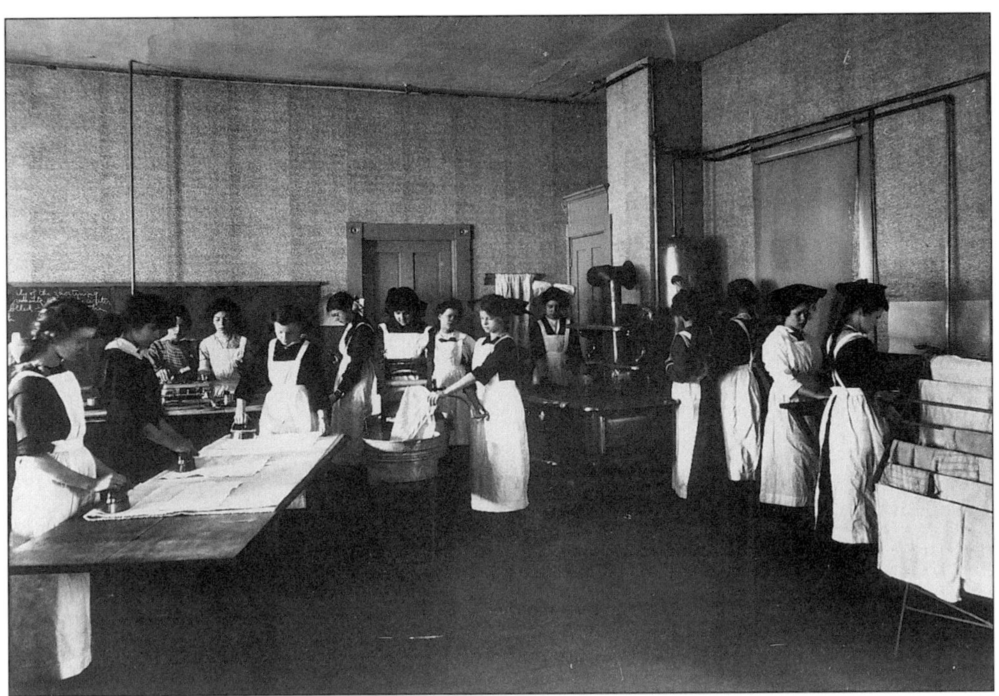

Dover Industrial School was located in the basement of the old City Hall. Classes were offered for both girls and boys, teaching skills such as drafting, woodworking, cooking and ironing. (Thom Hindle Collection.)

The Bear Island House, early 1900s. Originally this house was started as a boarding house by Mr. and Mrs. Leonard Davis in 1879. For many summers the fine hotel accommodated tourists from far and wide. In October 1934 it closed, and on November of that same year it burned to the ground. Its cellar hole can still be seen, about 1/4 mile inland from the P.O. dock on the north end of Bear Island. During its heyday, the hotel was operated by Grana Hatte Fay; Merrill Fay also ran this fine seasonal hotel for a time.

Governor Powell and Ed Downing, 1952. The governor came to view the boat races in Alton Bay. This particular boat is known as a Lyman Islander.

This 1875 photograph shows the Randall family and guests in North Conway.

Like many others, Jim and Addie Annis opened their Albany farm to hunters, trappers, and tourists. Jim subsidized the inn by driving stages, delivering mail, and breaking horses. The Annis farm was located at the end of the Bear Notch Road near what is now the Kancamagus Highway.

The Old Town Team on Meredith Bay, 1880s. The Shook Lumber Company can be seen on the right. The team was used to break roads throughout the town.

Albany: Girls from Pine Knoll Camp hiking Mt. Chocorua in the 1920s stop for a rest at the "shelter" which was located on the ledges on the back side of the mountain. The building, now long gone, was used as sleeping quarters by the fire wardens. (G. and R. Morrill.)

The M & M Food Store was also located in the King Building, as shown in this 1940s photograph, with Miss Liberty offering bakery samples. Liberty glasses were given free with a purchase. (Thom Hindle Collection.)

Winebaum's News was started in 1916 by Harry Winebaum, a sixteen-year-old newsboy. In the 1930s, Dover News operated from Depot Square on Third Street under the proprietorship of Thomas Winebaum, a wholesale news dealer. (T.H.C.)

The Soap Box Derby was once an annual event in Dover. Bruce Dearborn, the local winner in 1949, was off to the National in Akron, Ohio. (T.H.C.)

Loading Hubbard squash from the New Hampshire College farms, 1904.

"Pa" Taylor, Factator (chairman) of the Factato Club of Durham, dispensing refreshment to club members preparing to plant the potato crop, May 1917. The efforts of the Factaters, as the club members were known, produced 260 bushels of potatoes in 1917, and 324 bushels the following year.

Preparations for a clambake at the Colony Cove House near Little Bay, 1927

Old Spring Market on Ceres Street as it appeared *c.* 1870. Later the market became a ferry landing for the Portsmouth, Kittery, and York Street Railway in Portsmouth.

The north country girls were ready for the Berlin carnival, *c.* 1920. These are the right clothes for winter shopping, snowshoeing, skating, skiing, and carnival watching. After the Great War, women could wear sporting pants, rather than the long skirts of the earlier days.

A quiet scene amid the pines at Wacipi Pines in Center Barnstead, New Hampshire, 1935.

Race car No. 40, called the *Meredith Ford*, on Meredith Bay, Thanksgiving Day, 1951. Pictured are Tony Amabile (the driver) and his two children, Thomas (left) and Anthonette. According to the AP News, this vehicle was electrically timed at 90 mph, its top speed.

As with the shoe industry in Littleton, Ira Parker's glove business did not long remain alone; other plants were quickly established, one of them by two of his brothers, but all were finally merged into the Saranac Company. President Langford is shown here presenting pairs of their famous ski mitts (often called "tow-mitts" because they helped grip the slippery, wet rope of the first ski tows) to a visiting Chilean ski team.

The stage performances did not always run to heavy drama in Littleton. The "Pony Ballet" includes Fred and Frank Richardson, Fred English, Carter Nutting, Dr. Young, Hiram Gardner, Henry Peabody, and Harry Page Johnson, but for modesty's sake no attempt will be made to identify them further.

The toboggan slide at Gray's Inn in Jackson. In the 1920s, Gray's Inn opened part-time during the winter months for groups who wished to snowshoe and toboggan in the village.

The Crow's Nest at the base of the Jackson Falls in 1915 was a favorite spot for romance, long lunches, or just to watch the Wildcat River flow by.

The Stratham men's baseball team in 1903. Listed from left to right are as follows: (front row) Ralph Gowen and Ralph Barker; (second row) George Jewell, Jimmy Nixon, and ? Batchelder; (back row) Ridgely Marsh, Charles Gear, Clarence Gowen, Harry Smith, and Charles Grant. (SHS.)

The beautifully decorated coach of the Jackson Falls House and its team of six, with
employees and family members, compete in a coaching parade in Intervale, New

Hampshire, in 1894. The Jackson Falls House, as well as other hotels in the village, would send its coach to Glen and Intervale to pick up guests arriving at the rail stations.

When Bill and Betty Whitney purchased the Moody place in 1936, they renamed it Whitneys' in Jackson. Their specific interest was skiing, and in 1937 they ordered a number of shovel handles from Sears, Roebuck & Company and redesigned the lift using the handles to make it easier to ride. This bit of Yankee ingenuity remained until finally replaced in 1949.

George P. Trickey, the bachelor of the family, is on the left in this photograph of guests enjoying a "picturesque moment" on the porch of the original Jackson Falls House.

This silhouette captured Sherman Spears, a notable and distinguished ski jumper, in his first jump off the new Nansen Ski Jump in 1937. Unparalleled in bravery, jumpers of his caliber battled elements ranging from harsh wind currents to subzero temperatures. Kenneth Fysh and Leon Costello were also notable in this event, among many others.

This family enjoyed summer days at their cottage in a grove at the edge of Silver Lake, *c.* 1890. This and many other local lakes were convenient as summer retreats because of their close proximity to larger towns like Keene, and to rail lines from cities such as Boston.

This view on Hardscrabble Road in Swanzey showed the depths of the drifts and the work required to clear the roads after the famous blizzard of March 1888. It was six days after the storm that this cut, approximately 700 feet long, was opened through the drifts. Mr. Richardson inlaid the "1888" across the top of the arch with stones so the date of the "Great Blizzard" would never be forgotten.

"An Old Fashioned Lyceum" held at Melville Academy as one of the many Jaffrey sesqui-centennial events. At the far right is Mrs. Margaret Robinson, president of the Village Improvement Society for twenty years and the major force in the 1922 restoration of the Jaffrey Meetinghouse. Seventy years later another major restoration effort was taken on by the citizens of Jaffrey, demonstrating the same spirit and pride in their town's heritage. Melville Academy continues today as a restored schoolhouse and local history museum. (Jaffrey Center Village Improvement Society.)

Jaffrey's sesquicentennial celebration was a week-long affair. The parade was undoubtedly the highlight event. World War I having ended not long before, this contingent is probably made up of veterans; over one hundred Jaffrey men served their country in the conflict. (Jaffrey Historical Society.)

The postal sleigh at the Hancock Post Office in 1902. Charles Turner of Stoddard is the driver and in front of the door is the postmaster, Edgar Ware. The post office building is now a residence on Main Street. (Hancock Historical Society.)

It's difficult to image a prouder looking couple than the one pictured above. South Conway or "Goshen" families were noted both for their ingenuity and their rugged independence.

"Town Gathering." The Knights of Columbus staged this observance each year on Easter Monday from about 1908 to 1914 in Laconia. There was a big parade, most of it provided by the farmers—including all kinds of cattle, several hayracks carrying band members to provide music, and "a rube dressed to please the crowd." Each year people lined the streets looking forward to this event. In the evening, there were plays and dances. According to a notation on the back of the photograph, here are Michael J. Carroll, John M. Guay, James J. McCarthy, and Henry Johnson.

The town pump on Exeter Road, before 1900, in front of what is now Lamie's (see also p. 120). This popular horse-watering spot is being used by contractor Harry Brown (left) and Dr. Marvin Smith. The Howard G. Lane house at left was moved to 8 Dearborn Avenue when the railroad overpass was constructed in 1900. In this picture it stands approximately where the rear of Sanel Auto Parts is today. (Lane Memorial Library.)

Horace E. Rowen (1854–1934), Police and Truant Officer, on Mechanic Street in Lakeport. He was also the agent of the New Hampshire Woman's Humane Society, in which capacity he investigated complaints of cruelty to animals.

Two
BUSINESS

The Cheshire Tannery, founded by John Symonds in 1872, was located at the end of Symonds Place in Keene. Several large tanneries in the region prepared leather for use by other businesses such as shoe, harness, and trunk manufacturers. Seen here are four employees of the tannery in the 1870s.

Wilber's Meat Market wagons were ready to return to the streets several days after "The Great Storm" of March 1888. The "Blizzard of 1888" left 3 feet of snow in Keene. These drifts on Central Square were taller than the horses themselves. The gale force winds that accompanied the storm blew the snow into 15-foot drifts elsewhere in the region.

Blacksmith Peter Cote, a Canadian immigrant, in front of his shop on College Road, the road to Durham formerly known as Great Bridge Road since it connected the center of town to the bridge at the Squamscott. The shop is now a private home. At times there were four blacksmith shops in Stratham including one at 148 Portsmouth Avenue, one in the old trolley barn, one at the Gifford place, and one on Stratham Lane. (SHS.)

The Conway Lumber Company, *c.* 1910. On March 16, 1916, *The White Mountain Reporter* related the following: "Patrick Murphy fell over the guard fence on the saw mill slip and landed in a pile of snow about thirty feet below. A steam pipe broke his fall . . . Ike Tewksbury met with a peculiar loss last Sunday morning, while tending to his work as fireman at the big mill, he sneezed and a set of teeth were ejected from their usual resting place and found everlasting rest in the fire box."

A Redstone Quarry Crew. Many of the quarry workers were drifters moving from job to job. Others made Redstone their permanent home. Salaries for cutters ran about $9 per day, $3 more than for men working in the quarry.

With offices on the second floor of the Steamboat Hotel building, *The Farmington News* was a weekly newspaper originated by James E. Fernald and his son. First issued on March 14, 1879, it was published in this building until 1955.

Before the advent of automobiles, harness making was a profitable business as can be seen by this establishment on Main Street in Farmington.

The Old Corner Store in the 1890s in Laconia, operated by John Parker Smith. The former Gilford Academy building can be seen on the right.

Lavallee's Horse Boat operated on Lake Winnipesaukee from 1878 to 1890. The early boats used for transporting goods and people were barges. The gundalow was used somewhat, and some lumber schooners were said to have been used. The horse boat, with the horse or horses activating the side wheel paddles by means of a treadmill, was also used. However, even the most reliable horse boats did not fill the navigation needs of Lake Winnipesaukee.

The Belknap Savings Bank and Central House in Laconia, *c.* 1872, after the gabled roof replaced the original flat one. Located on the current site of the Sundial Shop, this building dates from 1831. Later, much expanded, the structure housed the Eagle Hotel, and was torn down in 1937 to make way for the new F.W. Woolworth store, which later became Benjamin's Clothing, and eventually the Sundial Shop.

South Tamworth, according to the Old Home Week 1906 booklet, John T.D. Folsom was appointed postmaster on May 11, 1846; either he or his wife (she was a Republican and he was a Democrat) ran the post office for over sixty years. For a few years the post office was in Elizabeth Maddox's house (now Lane's), but it returned to this building until 1959, when Carl Bickford opened the present post office. (Elva Bickford.)

J.W. Chamberlain's feed store and grain elevator operated until after World War II in Mountainview. It became Hickey's I.G.A. grocery store in 1965. In recent years it has housed various organizations. (Steve Damon.)

Masons marching to church in 1936. Since 1755, the Masons of Portsmouth and vicinity have observed the Feast of St. John the Baptist (June 24) almost every year by attending divine service at St. John's Church. This photograph shows a portion of the march as it passes from Middle Street to State Street.

The interior of the power station in the early 1900s in Laconia. Lewis Pierce is at the desk.

Cheshire Beef Company cattle on Main Street, April 13, 1911. Cattle were still herded through the street, despite increased trolley and auto traffic. Being a transportation hub meant that herds of animals would still be driven through Keene well into the twentieth century on their way to distant markets.

Sidney C. Ellis' West Keene Ice delivery wagon. The ice man was an important merchant in the days before refrigeration. Ellis, who operated West Keene Ice from 1901 to 1908, was one of three ice dealers in the city. Ice was cut in several local ponds for sale to city residents.

The Hamilton Smith Library. The new library was dedicated during commencement ceremonies, on June 3, 1907, although the building was not ready for use until November, and the relocation of the books from the town library was not complete until early in 1908. Gertrude Whittemore was appointed the first librarian under this new arrangement. Former town librarian Charlotte Thompson became the assistant librarian.

Interior of Tellers' Cage, Lakeport National Bank, c. 1917. The Mosler vault door was 12 inches thick and weighed 8 tons.

A BMT Patrol member heads out to groom the trails in Jackson. Extensive snow farming and grooming equipment operated all night if need be to keep snow properly packed. And the snow-making machinery on the J-Bar area was a further guarantee of good skiing throughout the winter.

After the hotel business began to decline, the Pequawket House in Conway Village survived for a while as a boarding house for workers from the Conway Lumber Company. Shown above is the bakery owned by John Shorey and Joseph Edwards, one of several businesses that were housed in the building. The Pequawket House was razed in 1923 to make room for Kennett High School.

Montgomery Ward and W.T. Grant Co. operated side by side for many years in Dover. Wards is now located at the Newington Mall, and when W.T. Grant Co. closed in October 1967, the space was occupied by Morton's Clothing Store.

George Leighton ran the Hotel Leighton, Leighton Barbershop, and Leighton's Lunch at 13 Third Street during the 1930s and '40s in Dover. It was famous for its Sunday 'One Dollar Turkey Dinners.'

With the growth of the settlements and the increase in the number of sawmills in Littleton, the demand for boards grew rapidly, and logging became the area's first industry. Most of the logging was done during the winter because dragging out the enormous logs was easier on ice and snow.

An interior view Ira Parker's glove manufactory showing the manufacturing process. It is interesting that the stitchers are mostly men, though a few female workers can be seen on the right in the background.

The Wentworth Hall management in Jacson, realizing the value of sanitary milk, built the most perfect pasteurizing plant in America. Guests were served fresh butter, and milk and cream in individually sealed bottles (or so this postcard by Walter Dole claims).

Littleton soon became a center for wood supply, as is illustrated by the size of Fred Dodge's operation in Apthorp (at the east end of town). Not only was lumber supplied as boards and timbers but these businesses eventually expanded into providing dimension lumber and finished millwork for homes far removed from the primitive log cabins of the early settlers, and in some ways, unmatched by the houses of today.

Some things never change!

Many a Farmington man was employed by Mooney's Mill during its fifty years of operation.

A typical shoe shop interior. Hattie White (on the far right) donated a large collection of town photographs to the library in Farmington.

A delivery cart leaving the Hayes factory in Farmington.

Progress comes to town! Main Street Farmington is paved at last by Harry Howard of Rochester and his road crew.

Prosperity arrived with the establishment of an auto dealership operated by John Ricker on Spring Street in Farmington.

The "New Mill" at Harrisville, built in 1867. It only stood for fifteen years, burning in 1882 under somewhat suspicious circumstances. This photograph shows the mill before a mansard roof was added to the tower. (JHS.)

Aime Tondreau was the mayor of Berlin and proprietor of Tondreau's Barbershop located on East Mason Street. During his tenure as mayor, his establishment became known as "City Hall" to many.

Three

ALONG THE SHORE

Britton's ferry, which connected Westmoreland with Putney, Vermont, unloaded passengers on the shore of the Connecticut River. Water travel has played a role in the region's history since the first settlers in Westmoreland arrived by canoe in the 1740s. Commercial navigation was attempted on the Ashuelot and Connecticut Rivers during the first half of the 19th century, before the railroad became the transportation mode of choice. The existence of Britton's ferry, and many others, proved that water was also an obstacle to travelers. These ferries transported passengers where the construction of bridges was impractical or too expensive. Britton's ferry met a tragic end when it sank in 1930, drowning four people.

The Ashuelot River has been used recreationally for well over a century. This view from 1889 shows boaters, fishermen, and sightseers all enjoying the river at the East Surry Road bridge, where the Ashuelot meanders through southern Surry before flowing into the city of Keene. A view of the river at the same location today might differ only in the degree of technology employed by those taking recreation. The fishing pole would be replaced by a rod and reel, the carriage by an automobile, and the rowboat by a canoe or kayak.

In addition to recreation, the river has played an important role in the county's industrial history. The Ashuelot flows through seven of the region's 23 communities and its water has powered dozens of mills as it moved from the northern border of the county to its confluence with the Connecticut River to the south.

A favorite swimming spot on the Squamscott near the Stratham town landing and the old Newfields bridge. These 1920 swimmers are Stanley French, Dorothy Pearson, some unknown legs, and Charles Hall. Mr. Hall lived in the house to the left of the bridge.

Hampton Beach, July 4, 1915.

When the keel snagged on the ways, stopping the launching of *Governor Endicott* on July 20, 1905, a rope was carried across the water and attached to a locomotive. "Two or three yanks were successful" and she "slid gracefully into the water." The steamer, which carried as many as 500 passengers, was dismantled at Lakeport in April 1928.

At first glance, one might mistake the 1861 wing dam (center left), which ran parallel with the river, for the Elm Street Bridge. The bridge, however, is obscured by the Lakeportgatehouse (right) and runs, of course, at a right angle to the river, from left to right.

A Coast Guard Station lifeboat, with passengers and crew. Despite the serious responsibilities shouldered by the crew of the station, there were few rescues to perform and they spent most of their time training and practicing. These exercises became a popular tourist attraction. (John Genthner and Arthur Moody)

The Mile Bridge and the Hampton River, looking west from White Rocks Island. The bridge was a toll road that made good money for its owners for many years. eventually, in 1933, it was purchased by the state, who continued to charge tolls. The wooden planding was a great fire hazard, and small fires caused by discarded cigarettes kept local firefighters busy, often several times a day during the busy summers. (Emile Dumont).

The Hampton Beach Casino, early 1900s. Before it was even two years old this new attraction drew thousands of vacationers to this long, wide, sandy stretch of beach that heretofore hadn't been as accessible. Nearly one hundred years later the Casino is still thriving. (ED)

Sawyer Pond (1,113 acres), sheltered on all sides by cliffs and mountain peaks, is nestled away from the rush of civilization in the towns of Livermore and Bartlett. It occupies a deep basin left by a retreating glacier. Forty-six acres in size, its crystal clear water reaches a depth of over 100 feet, with an average depth of 44 feet. The surrounding mountains are Tremont (alt. 3,371 feet), Owl Cliff (alt. 2,940 feet), and Green's Cliff (alt. 2,926 feet). Biologist Paul Hooper and a helper are shown here conducting the fish census of Sawyer Pond for the U.S. Fish and Wildlife Service, August 14–22, 1958.

The first Oceanic Hotel on Star Island. In the early 1870s, the last residents of the town of Gosport on Star Island sold out to hotel interests and the southern three islands of the Isles of Shoals were annexed to the Town of Rye.

Not all boats on the beach were wrecks! This boatload of maidens is in front of the Jenness Beach Lifesaving Station.

Main Street, Jaffrey, on September 21, 1938. The Jaffrey Mills are on the right. The bridge was not re-opened until the following year. (JHS)

The steamer *Limit*, a 45-foot tow boat with a 6-by-6 single-cylinder engine. The *Limit* was first owned by Emerson George, who is shown here at the wheel house, while Harry Caldwell, the world champion bicycle rider, stands by *Uncle Tom's Cabin*, c. 1930s. The dog's name is unknown.

Loading the Steamer Mount Washington at the Weirs Dock, 1920. This was a common sight: passengers with their luggage boarding the vessel for an excursion on Lake Winnipesaukee.

Littleton is indeed in many ways a "center" of the White Mountain region: business, cultural, and above all, scenic. Within a 50 mile radius are views that made the region one of the major tourist attractions in the country until the opening of the western mountains. For the last few pages of this book we have selected, more or less at random, a few of these scenes as frosting on the cake. In the above photograph, the mighty Connecticut River shows its muscle.

Steamer *Mineola*, c. 1885. Built at Newburg, New York, in 1877, she was shipped to Lakeport by rail in July of that year. "Probably no boat on the lake ever brought in as large dividends to its owners . . . She was the first steamer on the lake, large enough for freight and passenger business, to be fitted with a screw propeller."

Speed boats at Weirs Beach, late 1920s. These races were sponsored by Jim Irwin and the Winnipesaukee Power Boat Association with the active assistance of Sam Dunsford of Concord, and Archie Gulliford of "724 Cigar" fame in Manchester. These gentlemen made special arrangements with the driver by offering them free gas to run their race boats, and with the Boston & Maine Railroad to commute people from Boston to Weirs Beach for the races. This event was very popular for many years.

A rare photograph of Captain Lavallee, center with his white captain's hat, and John Goodhue at the helm, Paugus Bay, early 1930s.

The *Rip III* and Glen Scott, pilot. Here Jim Irwin, wearing a white hat, is seen judging the annual boat show at The Weirs. The young girl looking on is Dotty Irwin, 1935.

A bath scene on Long Pond (Lake Kanasatka), Moultonboro, NH. This charming lake is located one mile east of Center Harbor. The waters of this lake empty into Lake Winnipesaukee by a stream between the Second and Third Moultonboro Necks.

The Ames Station on the shore of Lake Winnipesaukee in Gilford, NH, 1935.

Three divers known as the "Swedish Luther League Fellows" doing their swan dive at Geneva Point Camp in Moultonboro, NH, 1940.

The Mill Road Bridge over the Oyster River, *c.* 1890.

An unidentified crew hauling bricks on the Oyster River near the mouth of Bunker Creek, *c.* 1890.

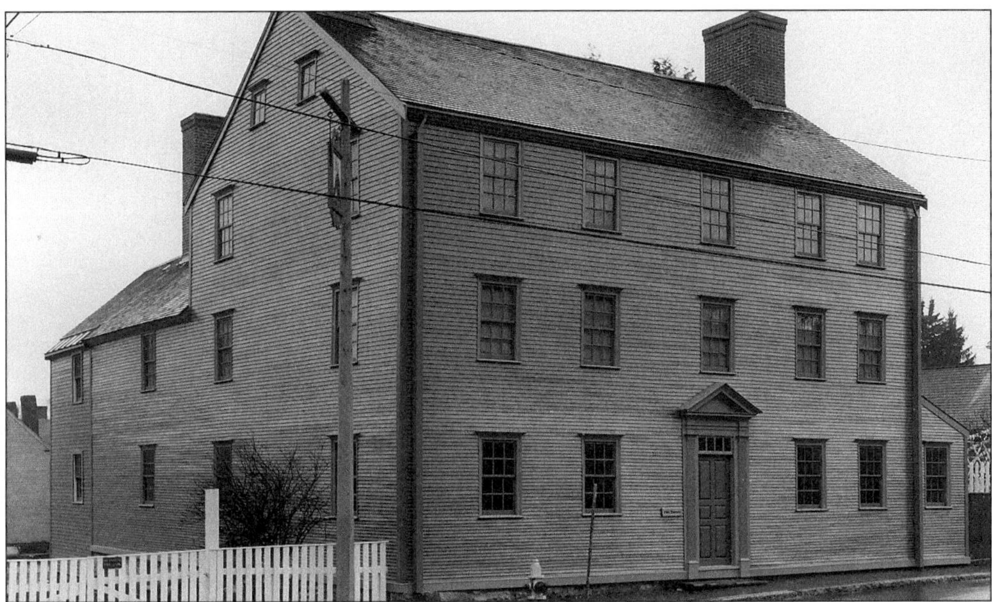

The William Pitt Tavern, originally known as the Earl of Halifax Tavern. This tavern was restored in 1987 by donations made by Freemasons of New Hampshire. The building is now owned by Strawbery Banke Museum, but the upper two stories are leased to the Grand Lodge of New Hampshire, F. & A.M. for 50 years.

The steamer *Lady of the Lake* at the Center Harbor dock, 1880s. This vessel was originally built by the Winnipesaukee Steamboat Company and launched at Lakeport, NH, in June 1849. She was the first lake passenger steamer and was operated under the ownership of the Boston, Concord and Montreal Railroad Company. She was retired from lake service in 1893. Her final resting place is located in 40 feet of water in Glendale Bay. Today, divers tell us that her hull is still in perfect condition.

The *Foxy* with the Tilton Players, 1950. This 42-foot wooden craft, owned by Carl and Amie Wallace, operated out of Paugus Bay, where Burger King is now located. The craft made daily excursions from Lakeport to The Weirs. From The Weirs it sailed among the Forty Islands, to Glendale, then under Governor's Island Bridge, and back to The Weirs, and finally to Lakeport, its home port.

The Shore Path at The Weirs, early 1900s.

Mr. Henry Law was present in August 1937 to dedicate the gift of a new outdoor pool to the city of Durham. (T.H.C.)

Two of the entertainers as they perform their antics in the Wentworth swimming pool in Jackson. The Wentworth Hall management was constantly bringing in different acts to entertain and amuse the vacationing guests.

The swimming pool of the Wentworth Hall, below the Solarium, served the resort well for many years. Every fall the Solarium was dismantled and then reassembled the following summer. There were many times over the years, after a downpour, that parts would wash away with the rapid and surging waters from the Jackson Falls. Many of the original pilings and foundations can still be seen amid the lower falls.

Dalton, just above Littleton, lies across the Connecticut River from Lunenburg, Vermont, and as the river is fairly broad here, a ferry is more affordable, if less useful, than a bridge. It is not known if the dog was a passenger in the car or regularly oversaw the operation of the ferry.

Four

TO SERVE AND PROTECT

The veterans of the 14th Regiment returned to Winchester for a reunion in September of 1886, 24 years after they broke camp in the town. The 14th Regiment served in several major battles during the Civil War, including Winchester, Virginia, Opequan, Fishers Hill, and Cedar Creek.

The ladder truck of the Laconia Fire Department in Depot Square in the early 1900s.

A World War I parade passes through Bank Square in Laconia. O'Shea's (in the Moulton Opera House Block) is on the right.

The Farmington Fire Department was originally composed of two companies: the Hook and Ladder Company and the Engine Company. The Hook and Ladder men in this 1860 picture were a colorful group with their gray uniforms trimmed with red, white, and blue stripes.

Firemen muster in Bank Square, 1888, with an Amoskeag steamer, hose wagons, and a hook and ladder. The Laconia National Bank building is under construction, between the Unitarian Church and Truland Bros. (right). From 1889–1903, the Laconia Public Library was located in the bank building.

The 20 members of the Deluge Hose Company posed with their hose wagon in front of the fire station, *c.* 1890. Keene's two hose companies and one hook and ladder company had a total of 65 members.

CARL E. WALLACE, AGE 16, LATER PROPRIETOR OF THE FOXY EXCURSION BOATS, AT REINS OF LAKEPORT'S HOSE CO. 4 WAGON. The Adams-Moulton House at 743 Union Avenue (in the background) still exists with its outbuildings, between today's Lake Village Apartments high-rise and the Robbins Auto Parts store.

Here the Niagra Engine House of Gold Street in Lakeport is labeled LVFD, with two entrances—Niagara on the left and the Hook & Ladder Co. on the right. Henry Odell's Gold Street clothing store is at right. Firemen in full regalia and city officials pose in front of the hook & ladder wagon.

Dr. Herbert W. Drury's fire boat. In 1965, Captain Drury of Tuftonboro Neck is seen in this trim craft equipped with four custom-built nozzles which are powered by two nine-h.p. Gurham-Rupp pumps with an output of 310 gallons per minute. This craft can send a stream 150 feet in any direction. The apparatus is mounted on a 22-foot fiberglass hull, drawing 27 inches of water. Propelled by a 90 h.p. marine engine, the vessel can reach speeds of up to 25.6 knots.

Police Chief Louis Bourgoin (third from left) and other police officers at a 1935 UNH track meet in durham. Bourgoin began working at the college in 1918 as a janitor and part-time night policeman. In addition to serving as a full-time campus policeman, the town later hired him as police chief, a post he held from 1928 through 1955.

Marshall Benjamin Hall and constables William Philbrick and Robert Tolman posed in front of Keene City Hall, c. 1905. Marshall Hall reported 95 arrests for the four-month period ending March 1, 1905; 83 were for drunkenness.

Police Officers Fretch and Bailey, mid-1890s, Lakeport, New Hampshire. In the upper right corner, past the Cole Manufacturing Co. buildings, the stair tower of the Halifax Mill is visible.

The veterans of the 14th Regiment returned to Winchester for a reunion in September of 1886, 24 years after they broke camp in the town. The 14th Regiment served in several major battles during the Civil War, including Winchester, Virginia, Opequan, Fishers Hill, and Cedar Creek.

Attendees of a Grand Army of the Republic reunion pose in Central Square in Keene, *c.* 1895. This patriotic association composed of Union veteran soldiers, sailors, and marines was founded in 1866; the John Sedgwick Post, No. 4 in Keene was formed in 1868. This large gathering may have taken place in commemoration of the 30th anniversary of the end of the Civil War.

A squad of cavalry on drill at Camp Natt Head (so named for New Hampshire's governor) in 1879. The Keene Light Guard Battalion hosted the New Hampshire National Guard at this four-day encampment at the Cheshire Fairgrounds (now Wheelock Park). Guard units such as these served as the local military presence for several decades after the Civil War.

The Hampton Police Department, 1915. Hampton's force consisted of only four officers at this time. In the front row, from left to right are Chief Robert Tolman, police "mascot" Wendell "Buster" Ring, Edward MacFarland, Uri Lamprey, Ray Haselton, and John Clark (of Nashua). During the big carnival week in September extra officers were brought in from Keene and Nashua. The men in back are unidentified, although one is Officer Gilbo of Keene. (Tuck Museum.)

Built in 1865, the Orchard Street Station (now the Firehouse Restaurant) was considered one of the neatest, coziest and best equipped engine houses in the state at the turn of the century. (T.H.C.)

Above, a hose crew streams water from the roof of the boiler house to cool the ruins. Below, ice covers the walls on the end of the ell of Mill No. 1, known today as the Clarostat Mill. (T.H.C.)

The crew of the Wallis Sands Lifesaving Station *c.* 1900 in Rye. Captain Frank Wells, John Pridham, Horace Berry, Ben Ricker, and Thomas Varrell have been identified.

The 1905 wreck of the *Lizzie Carr* off Concord Point, with a dramatic rescue by the Wallis Sands crew in progress. The first mate drowned in the attempt but six crewmen were rescued.

Local lifesavers practicing with the breeches buoy.

Camp Samoset in Gilford, New Hampshire, 1937. Water safety was always an important activity at camp. Here the life guard is seen conducting a safety class on the camp's dock. In 1939, Camp Samoset, founded by Thomas E. Freeman, celebrated its 25th anniversary. The camp was later sold to Manny Winston, who operated it from 1944 to 1968. Samoset was named after the only red-headed Native American ever known to have existed in this area. Today this is the site of the Samoset Condominiums on Route 11, Gilford, New Hampshire.

Farmington has a long history of Boy Scouting going back to 1912. These 1922 Scouts were led by Scoutmasters Leslie Ham and Norman Davis.

The crew of the second Jenness Beach Lifesaving Station, built in 1890. Captain Albert Remick is at the stern.

Peterborough's Tarbell Block on the corner of Main and Grove Streets was heavily damaged by fire on December 7, 1902. It was renovated with an extra two floors added and is now known as the Granite Block. (Peterborough Historical Society.)

The Peterborough fire department in the early 1900s in front of "Aquarius," probably at a firemen's muster. The letter A on their uniforms is for Aquarius which was the early name of the fire company before it became a department of town government. (PHS)

Five
FUN AND GAMES

A baseball game behind the Casino in Hampton, c. 1908. (ED).

A girls' race at the Remick Park rink in Littleton, perhaps in conjunction with the Winter Carnival, draws a number of spectators.

A group of Outing Club members at Bridal Veil Falls on the western slope of Cannon (Profile) Mountain. This is a fairly stiff climb of some 2.5 miles from the highway (Route 116). One wonders if the dog is regretting not having brought an extra jacket.

This 1924 "happening" in Farmington was recorded by the famous photographer and author, Wallace Nutting. The young gentleman in knee britches standing next to his mother is James E. Thayer.

This Main Street establishment was where some of the boys spent their time before the days of video arcades.

A great variety of clubs existed in the early 1900s as a focus of social life. Seen here are members of the Montauk Club in front of the Opera House.

The Farmington High School baseball team, *c.* 1903.

The 1925 high school girls basketball team consisted of: (front row) Evelyn Otis, Rhuma Hayes, Molly Stanley, Beatrice Perkins, and Pauline Hayes; (back row) Beatrice Hartfield, Norma Brown, Dorothy Burbank, Evelyn Parker, and Ruth Webster.

The Contoocook Singing Orchestra of East Jaffrey. The leader and cornetist was Alfred L. Towne. Beginning in 1903 the band, composed mostly of family members, performed several times a week at gatherings throughout the region. It disbanded in 1932. (JHS)

The 1968 World Champion Sled Dog Race in Laconia, New Hampshire. Sled dog races continue to be an exciting winter activity of the Lakes Region.

The club of 1876 is nattily attired in monogrammed shirts and fancy socks. They are, from left to right: (seated) Shepard, 2B; Tuttle, P; Van Houten, C; and Chase, 3B; (standing) Cochrane, 1B; George, CF; Johnson, RF; Byron, LF; and Parker, SS. (B.W. Kilburn, Ltn.)

After a hard day on the slopes, the many skiers at Whitneys' in Jackson relaxed by playing cards, board games, reading in the library, or carrying on discussions that were certain to solve the problems of the world.

A children's group known as the "Rainbow Minstrels" entertains at the Opera House in 1925 in Littleton. From left to right are Nichol D. Cragie, Effie Simons Willey, Elliot Mason, Mary Childs Miner, Louise Nute Peabody, Mary Sweeney, John Semanik, Lawrence Colby, and Marion Morrison Davis.

A baseball game on a summer afternoon in 1886 in Rye. Included in this group are at least three of the Englishmen who manned the local telegraph cable station. Those identified are William Fraser, John Fraser, Patrick Reib, and George Brown.

Grace Fowler Newcomb, Kitty Smith, and Alice Goodnow dressed up as gypsies for a hospital fund raiser in 1921 in Keene. The fair, featuring exotic dancers, freaks of nature, and a parade, was a success, as was the hospital campaign itself. The result was a modern sixty-bed medical wing at the Elliot Hospital.

Margaret and Ralph Whitcomb enjoying a day of play on West Street in the mid-1890s. Elaborate children's toys, such as this wonderful Victorian tricycle, illustrate the increased purchasing power of the middle class. The railroad repair shops dominated the horizon.

A well-attended ball game on Apthorp Common, *c.* 1880. The fine home on the right is that of H.C. Redington, associated with the scythe manufacturing and lumber businesses in Apthorp.

Sewall's Point, Wolfeboro, New Hampshire, 1908. This point was named after Judge David Sewell, an attorney-at-law from Portsmouth, New Hampshire. According to public records, this property was owned by Judge Sewell at the time of its settlement.

Tamworth: This wonderful picture was, of course, taken at Ordination Rock, but the date and the names of the tennis players are unknown. Mary Trask, Barnstormers' expert costumer, places it at around the turn of the century. She also noted that both young men have wide belts with snake buckles—perhaps a clue to a college or club? (Tamworth Historical Society.)

Possibly the greatest social event in Littleton's history occurred in April 1941 when movie star Bette Davis came here to celebrate her birthday and be present at the premiere showing of her latest film *The Great Lie*. Eager crowds await the star's arrival at the train station.

THE STAGE OF LIFE

This noisy and cumbersome steam roller used for road maintenance was operated by Harry Knox (in hat).

This Farmington High School class trip to Washington, D.C., took place in 1931. My, haven't fashions changed!

Was this jolly group an outdoor dining club or just well-dressed sportsmen-campers?

Although weighing several tons this large block of Marlborough granite does not seem to strain the wagon in the least. (Marlborough Historical Society.)

Baskets are still produced in Peterborough. This extra large one was made by the Needham Basket Company sometime after 1906 when the business moved into the former piano factory on Depot Street. (PHS)

The notation on the back of this snapshot reads "Probably the first auto wreck in Jaffrey, on the Ark Road." The car on the right labeled "Dillon" may have been that of Edward or Oscar Dillon, father and son, who ran an auto livery service for many years. (JHS)

The stone store and Mead's Tavern in Chesterfield Center are shown here around 1870. Levi Mead, a veteran of the Revolutionary War, built Mead's Tavern in 1816. The tavern, also known as the Chesterfield Hotel, later burned. Asa March built the stone store in 1849. Two years later his nephew Benjamin, a native of Chesterfield, formed the firm "Jordan, Marsh & Co." with Eben Jordan of Boston.

A coaching parade entry pauses before the Whitaker homestead in North Conway. The parades were popular diversions for hotel guests and a favorite spectacle for locals.

Once the summer home of Frances White Bucher, Pine Knoll Camp for girls in nearby Albany was sold around 1940 and converted to a boys camp. Here, campers exercise in their brown serge middy blouses and bloomers. Boys' and girls' camps offered a bucolic retreat, replete with arts, crafts, and nature study. Similar camps still dot the countryside.

The Fitchburg #246 derailed at Pemberton Crossing in West Keene on July 17, 1897. Engineer Milan Curtis died when two locomotives and five freight cars of this hog train left the tracks. Train travel was not without its dangers. Then, as now, such wrecks drew large crowds of curious spectators.

Keene's road crew proudly displays the city's modern road paving equipment in this view from the 1880s. Keene acquired such technological developments as the city grew and prospered and residents demanded municipal improvements. It would be several decades before some of the region's declining smaller towns could afford such "luxuries." This view was taken on Court Street with the Second Congregational Church at the right.

116

Raising the flagpole at Stratham Hill Park on Old Home Day, August 1908. Shown here are Bert Burbank, George E. Gowen, Eddie Tuttle, Arthur Jewell, Melvin Stickney, Levi Prentiss Wiggin, J.C. Piper, and Gilbert Thompson. The old growth pine mast was cut from Mrs. Josiah B. Wiggin's lot and shaped by a spar maker from the Portsmouth Naval Shipyard. Ralph Laighton, a Portsmouth bank president who had lived in Stratham, donated the flag. (SHS.)

Arthur Jewell on a cart with a donkey on Winnicutt Road. (SHS.)

An 80-pound striped bass caught by Albert West in Stratham, *c.* 1910. (SHS.)

The removal of the Cooke Elm from West Street in March 1914. The tree stood on this location for more than 140 years. As West Street was widened during the nineteenth century, vehicles passed on either side of the tree. The advent of the automobile finally doomed this prominent landmark.

118

Mercury vapor street lights transformed night into day when they were installed on Keene's Main Street in 1953. This 4:20 am view shows a deserted downtown. Long-time Main Street businesses such as the Monadnock Grill, Crystal, and Bon Ton restaurants, and Fishman's, Newberry's, and Woolworth's department stores would unlock their doors in a few hours. The national entertainment industry had a Main Street presence by this time: Clark Gable was appearing in *Mogambo* at the Latchis Theatre.

Paving Court Street in the late 1880s in Keene. The city itself has been a major employer for more than a century. Building and maintaining streets, water systems, sewers, cemeteries, and other public assets requires considerable manpower. This view reveals the road building technology of the late nineteenth century. A large wood-fired steam engine powers a rock crusher as two supervisors sit on an elaborate dump wagon. Visible at the right is the Second Congregational Church.

The wreck of the Fitchburg #246 at West Keene, July 17, 1897. Two locomotives and five freight cars of this hog train derailed at West Keene, resulting in the death of engineer Milan Curtis, and many hogs. Such wrecks drew large crowds of curious bystanders, including at least nineteen who came by bicycle to view this derailment.

The trolley on the Swanzey Factory run slid off the snowy rails on Keene's lower Main Street in 1910. New England winters posed the same challenges to rail vehicles that they do to automobiles.

Pulling down the Unitarian Church steeple, 10:32 am, January 29, 1894, Keene, New Hampshire. This remarkable shot chronicled the demise of this longtime Main Street landmark. Its replacement, the Unitarian Church on Washington Street, was dedicated in January 1895.

This was the golden wedding anniversary party of Dauphin and Ruth (Mason) Wilson (seated) on November 3, 1886, in Keene. Dauphin Wilson was a farmer, carpenter, schoolteacher, poet, justice of the peace, and one of the most influential men in his native town of Sullivan. This group of Sullivan representatives gathered to celebrate the couple's anniversary. Dauphin and Ruth had no children to share the celebration; their only child, a son, died 49 years earlier at the age of two days.

An airplane on Hampton Beach, c. 1920. Stunt flying and airplane rides were a fewquent attraction at Hampton Beach during the first years of this century, beginning with the first Carnival Week in 1915. (LML).

Mudbuggy racers lined up to start a Sunday afternoon of racing on Meredith Bay. From left to right are Brad Bryant, Tot Dearborn, Bryan Avery (captain of the MV *Mount Washington*), Vin Callahan, William Young, and Tony Amabile.

The fanciful float of L.J. Merchand & Co., shoe dealer. Around the turn of the century, commerce and industry vied for the most imaginative floats in the frequent parades.

President William Howard Taft addresses the citizens of Lisbon in the town square.

Although generally popular at Rye's local socials, one reporter thought that "sick elephants would sound more delightful" after hearing one of the Spear's Brass Band's rehearsals.

On the steps of the Sea View House in Rye. It is interesting to realize that although behavior and morals were important in the Victorian era, the high-class resorts included a lot of young people and youthful activities.

The steam train No. 122 of the Lake Shore Railroad at the Glendale Station, 1897. The railroad began operation from Alton Bay to Lake Village (Lakeport/Laconia) in 1890 and ended in 1930. In 1933 the tracks were removed.

Wealthy Victorian visitors to Rye Beach would bring or hire a governess for the children. An 1871 brochure for the Ocean House states that children with adult appetites would be charged accordingly.

Yankee ingenuity at work following the hurricane in Littleton in September 1938. Without electricity to operate the gas pump, bicycle-power is substituted.

Mr. Meeker weighing his pig, part of a program operated through UNH Cooperative Extension, 1925.